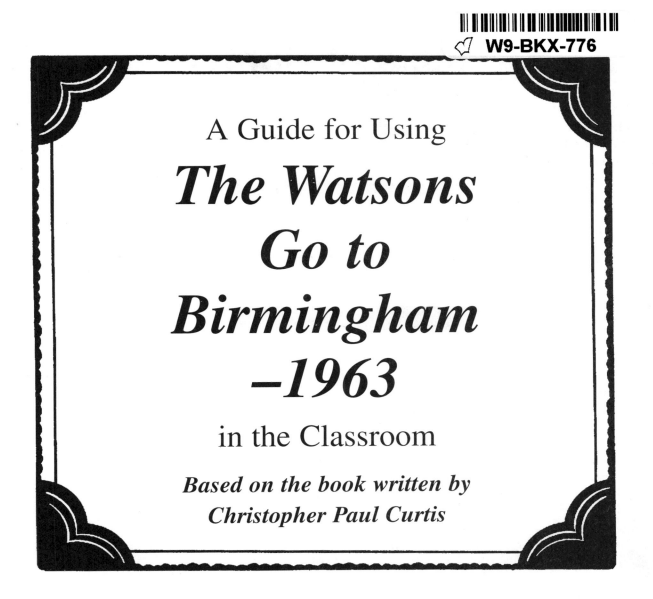

A Guide for Using

The Watsons Go to Birmingham –1963

in the Classroom

Based on the book written by
Christopher Paul Curtis

This guide written by **Debra J. Housel, M.S. Ed.**

Teacher Created Materials, Inc.
6421 Industry Way
Westminster, CA 92683
www.teachercreated.com
©2002 Teacher Created Materials
Made in U.S.A.
ISBN 0-7439-3155-6

Edited by
Eric Migliaccio

Illustrated by
Kevin Barnes

Cover Art by
Brenda DiAntonis

Table of Contents

Introduction

A novel as entertaining as *The Watsons Go to Birmingham—1963* makes the issues of racism and the Civil Rights movement of the early 1960s both real and relevant to today's students. Christopher Paul Curtis helps his readers to experience childhood in the early 1960s through the voice of Kenny Watson, a 10-year-old African-American boy.

The Watsons Go to Birmingham—1963 provides many opportunities for students to discuss the difficulties of growing up. Not only will this literature unit entertain, it will provide a wealth of teachable moments. Teachers who use this unit will find the following features:

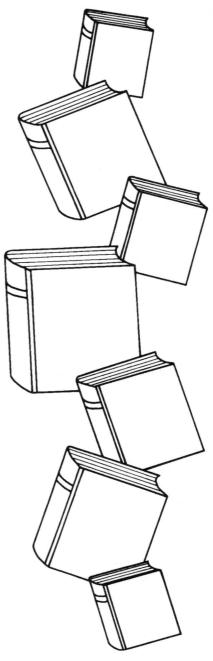

- A Sample Lesson Plan
- Pre-reading Activities
- A Biographical Sketch of the Author
- A Book Summary
- Vocabulary Lists by Section
- Vocabulary Activity Ideas
- Chapters of the book grouped by sections, each of which include the following:

  —quizzes
  —hands-on projects
  —cooperative-learning opportunities
  —cross-curricular activities
  —writing lessons
  —connections to relate to the reader's own life

- Post-reading Activities, including:
  —book report ideas
  —culminating activities

- Three Different Options for Unit Tests:
  —objective (matching and true/false/explain)
  —explaining quotes from the book
  —conversations (students write conversation scripts for characters)
- Bibliography of Related Readings
- Answer Keys

This literature unit will be an invaluable addition to your literature planning. By using these ideas, your students will discover the delightful companionship to be found in a good book, while learning about an important historical event in an engaging, thought-provoking way.

Sample Lesson Plans

Each of the lessons suggested below can take between one and three days to complete. You can adapt the lessons to meet the needs of your students.

Lesson 1
1. Complete some or all of the pre-reading activities (page 5).
2. Read "About the Author" to your students (page 6).
3. Introduce the vocabulary for section 1 (page 8).
4. Initiate some of the Vocabulary Activity Ideas (page 9).
5. Read chapters 1–4.

Lesson 2
1. Discuss section 1 (chapters 1–4).
2. Do quiz time for section 1 (page 10).
3. Begin a reader's response journal (page 14).
4. Study dinosaurs (page 11).
5. Learn about the Empire State Building (page 12).
6. Read Greek myths (page 13).
7. Introduce vocabulary for section 2 (page 8).
8. Read chapters 5–8.

Lesson 3
1. Discuss chapters 5–8.
2. Do quiz time for section 2 (page 15).
3. Write a journal entry for chapters 5–8.
4. Begin creating a character study of a family member (page 16).
5. Locate sensory images in the text (page 17).
6. Write music critiques (page 18).
7. Invent portmanteau words (page 19).
8. Introduce vocabulary for section 3 (page 8).
9. Read chapters 9–11.

Lesson 4
1. Discuss chapters 9–11.
2. Do quiz time for section 3 (page 20).
3. Write a journal entry for chapters 9–11.
4. Create the Brown Bomber (page 21).
5. Make cartoon strips (page 22).
6. Identify figurative language (page 23).
7. Learn to use a road atlas (page 24).
8. Introduce vocabulary for section 4 (page 8).
9. Read chapters 12 and 13.

Lesson 5
1. Discuss chapters 12 and 13.
2. Do quiz time for section 4 (page 25).
3. Write a journal entry for chapters 12 and 13.
4. Assemble a jackdaw (page 26).
5. Do creative review questions activity (page 27).
6. Do the library research activity (page 29) prior to learning about weather (page 28).
7. Introduce vocabulary for section 5 (page 8).
8. Read chapters 14–15 and the epilogue.

Lesson 6
1. Discuss chapters 14–15 and the epilogue.
2. Do quiz time for Section 5 (page 30).
3. Write a journal entry for chapters 14–15.
4. Share the story's main events from each character's viewpoint by making character portraits (page 31).
5. Form literature circles (page 32).
6. Complete math word problems (page 33).
7. Compare yourself to Kenny or Byron (page 34).
8. Begin a culminating project (page 37).

Lesson 7
1. Discuss the entire book with the students and get their reaction to it.
2. Complete the family member character study project.
3. Assign book reports (page 35).
4. Discuss the history of the Newbery Medal (page 36).
5. Continue working on a culminating project.
6. Choose one or more test formats to evaluate your students' learning (pages 38–40).

Lesson 8
1. Complete the culminating project; do presentations.
2. Discuss test responses.

Before the Book

Before you read *The Watsons Go to Birmingham—1963* with your students, do some pre-reading activities to stimulate the students' interest and enhance their comprehension. Here are some activities and discussion questions for use with your class:

1. Ask the students to look at the book's cover and predict what the story will be about. Record these predictions on butcher paper and keep them posted during the unit. Have the students refer to their predictions occasionally throughout the literature unit to compare their pre-reading ideas to what actually happens in the story.

2. Discuss Dr. Martin Luther King, Jr. and his policy of non-violent protest.

3. On a piece of chart paper, brainstorm any information the students know about the Civil Rights movement and the 1960s. Discuss what caused the Civil Rights movement and how the people met in churches and formed peaceful demonstration marches under the guidance of Dr. Martin Luther King, Jr. Help the students to get a feel for the times and appreciate the importance of music at the mass meetings and marches by playing songs from these CDs: *Voices of the Civil Rights Movement: Black American Freedom Songs 1960–1966*, performed by various folk groups (audio CD—2 discs), Smithsonian Folkways, 1997. AISN B000001DJT) and *Sing for Freedom: The Story of the Civil Rights Movement Through Its Songs*, performed by various folk groups (audio CD—1 disc), Smithsonian Folkways, 1993. AISN: B000001DHL).

4. Examine the novel's key themes: bullies, death, and the evil of racism. Have the students explore these issues by using the following questions in a class discussion:
   - Have you ever had an encounter with a bully? Elaborate.
   - What are some things that bullies do to other people?
   - What do you think causes a person to act like a bully?
   - How can you help someone who is a victim of a bully?
   - Have you ever had a near-death experience? Explain.
   - Have you ever heard about someone else's near-death experience? What happened?
   - What is racism?
   - What are some acts of racism?
   - How can you help someone who is a victim of racism?
   - How can you prevent racism?

5. Watch the documentary *Four Little Girls* by Spike Lee (HBO Home Video, 2000). This 102-minute film about the September 15, 1963, church bombing is available in VHS and DVD formats and provides a powerful account of the events leading up to as well as the aftermath of the bombing of the Sixth Street Baptist Church Sunday school in Birmingham, Alabama.

6. Listen to the song "Birmingham Sunday," available on *Joan Baez/5* performed by Joan Baez (audio CD (1 disc) or audiocassette, Vanguard, 1989. AISN: B000000EHY). Joan Baez, a popular folk singer in the 1960s and 1970s, recorded this song about that tragic morning when Cynthia Wesley, Denise McNair, Carole Robertson, and Addie Mae Collins lost their young lives.

7. Read aloud to your class the poem that inspired Christopher Paul Curtis to write this novel. It is entitled "The Ballad of Birmingham," and it was written by the late Detroit Poet Laureate Dudley Randall. The poem is a part of a young-adult anthology entitled *In Search of Color Everywhere: A Collection of African American Poetry*, edited by E. Ethelbert Miller, Stewart Tabori, & Chang Publishers, 1996 (paperback) or Econo-Clad Books, 1999 (hardcover). It may also be found online. See the bibliography on page 43 of this guide.

About the Author

Born in 1954, Christopher Paul Curtis grew up in Flint, Michigan. Curtis says that he and his sister grew up under the guidance of caring parents. He states, "My parents were both very demanding and very concerned that we do well, that we know right from wrong, and that we take care of business."

After graduating from high school, Curtis worked for 13 years on an automobile assembly line. He hung car doors on every other car at the Fisher Body Plant No. 1, the place where the United Auto Workers Union was born. One day, he and a co-worker agreed to double up so that they would each get half of every hour off. Curtis looked forward to these breaks because he would use them to write. Writing helped him to escape from the factory work, which he didn't enjoy. While working at the factory, he also attended the University of Michigan.

In 1993 his wife encouraged him to take an unpaid year's leave of absence to write his first novel. He originally planned to write the book as a lighthearted look at a loving, realistic black family in the 1960s. Then his son brought home a poem entitled "The Ballad of Birmingham" from school. After reading it, Curtis knew where he wanted to take the story: he wanted to show the dangers of being a black family in the 1960s—especially if you lived in the South.

He worked on *The Watsons Go to Birmingham—1963* night and day. Finally, he sent in his manuscript to a contest sponsored by Delacorte Press. He didn't win. However, the publisher was impressed with his work and decided to print it. His first book won a half-dozen awards, including the prestigious Newbery Honor and the Coretta Scott King Honor awards. Curtis's career as an author took off, and his days at the auto assembly plant were over.

His second novel, *Bud, Not Buddy*, won the Newbery Award and the Coretta Scott King Award in 1999. He is currently writing its sequel. Curtis has been praised because his novels appeal to people of all races. Curtis says, "If you're telling a good story, people will like it." In addition, he gets his readers get so involved with the characters that they feel as if they experienced a historical event with the characters. In his own words, "I think fiction can make history more immediate, more personal."

Today Curtis lives with his wife, Kaysandra, and their children, Steven and Cydney, in Windsor, Ontario, Canada. He loves working full-time as a children's writer because, as he says, "There is something nice about having a kid come up to you and say, 'I really liked your book.'"

The Watsons Go to Birmingham—1963

by Christopher Paul Curtis

(Bantam Doubleday Dell Books for Young Readers)

(Available in CAN, Bantam Doubleday Dell; UK, Doubleday Dell Seal; & AUS, Transworld)

As the middle child in a family of five, 10-year-old Kenny Watson tells us the story of his family, "the Weird Watsons," who live in Flint, Michigan. Most of Kenny's problems stem from his older brother, Byron, who is also the school bully. Now that Byron is 13, Kenny dubs him "officially a juvenile delinquent." The book begins in winter with some humorous adventures. Self-absorbed Byron gives his reflection a kiss and ends up with his lips frozen to the side-view mirror on the family car. Later Byron convinces Kenny and their kindergarten-aged sister, Joetta, that people with Southern blood freeze in their tracks and are hauled away in garbage trucks early each morning.

In addition to making trouble for Kenny, Byron is constantly in trouble himself. He frequently skips school; gets involved in fights; defiantly lights matches in the house; and gets his hair straightened into a "conk," even though he knows it will infuriate his parents. By the end of the school year, the Watson parents decide that only strict Grandma Sands can shape up Byron and teach him some sense. After Dad comes home with a car stereo system called the Ultra-Glide, the Watsons set out on a road trip to Grandma Sands' home in Birmingham, Alabama. They have no idea that they're about to experience a tragic moment in American history.

In Birmingham, Kenny faces death, racism, and evil for the first time. Kenny disobeys orders not to go to a swimming hole that has a whirlpool. Pulled under by the terrifying creature he calls the "Wool Pooh," he practically drowns, being saved at the last moment by Byron. The Wool Pooh is a powerful symbol of fear and death.

The Wool Pooh makes its second terrifying appearance after the bombing of the Sixteenth Avenue Baptist Church, where four girls are killed. (This is based on an actual event.) Joetta is attending Sunday school at the church. Fortunately, she has a mysterious hallucination of Kenny urging her to follow him and leaves the church building just before the bomb goes off. Not realizing this, Kenny rushes to the church to search through the rubble for his beloved little sister. The reader is carried along on the wave of Kenny's grief, for he believes that Joetta has been killed and that the evil Wool Pooh has her in its cold, gray clutches.

Even though Joetta is safe, after the family returns to Flint, Kenny experiences a severe depression and hides behind the family's couch. Surprisingly, it is Byron who gets him to come out and promises Kenny that he'll be all right. Curtis skillfully leads the reader through the development of the brothers' complex relationship.

Vocabulary Lists

On this page are vocabulary lists that correspond to each section. Vocabulary activity ideas can be found on page 9 of this book.

Section 1 (Chapters 1–4)

automatically	juvenile delinquent
blizzard	miraculous
cockeye	panning
demonstration	passionate
egghead	pomade
emulate	punctual
flypaper	reinforcements
frostbite	skimpy
grenade	thermostat
hambone	version
hostile	vital
hypnotized	zombie
incapable	

Section 2 (Chapters 5–8)

antifreeze	maestro
chihuahua	peon
cologne	pinnacle
conscience	seniority
cussing	Siam
dispersal	strangling
executioner	symphonic
flamethrower	technician
haphazardly	traitor
high-fidelity	udders
interpretations	ultimate
jive	Western civilization
linoleum	

Section 3 (Chapters 9–11)

accustomed	peninsula
eavesdropped	rabies
facilities	rednecks
gnashing	sanitation
hillbilly music	sheik
jive songs	snitch
pathetic	temptations

Section 4 (Chapters 12–13)

duking	trespassing
electrocuted	whirlpool
stingy	wilier

Section 5 (Chapters 14–15 & Epilogue)

boycotts	provoke
confrontations	quest
discrimination	raising Cain
interracial	seamstress
Magnolia tree	segregation
pervasive	sonic boom
picketing	strove
prohibited	

Vocabulary Activity Ideas

Help your students learn and retain the vocabulary used in *The Watsons Go to Birmingham—1963* by providing them with interesting activities, such as the following:

1. Word searches and crossword puzzles are fun for all ages. Students can use the vocabulary words from the story to create puzzles individually or in teams. Have them exchange papers and solve one another's puzzles. When the papers are completed, the authors can correct them.

2. Encourage the use of vocabulary words by making them your weekly spelling words. Writing sentences or paragraphs is also an effective way to expand usage.

3. A television news broadcast is a great way to give the students experience using vocabulary words. Put the students into groups of no more than four students. Assign each student a job in the "studio": anchor, co-anchor, producer, and meteorologist. Have them use the vocabulary words to create news stories. Encourage them to use as many vocabulary words in context as possible. Have each team present a broadcast to the class. As they present, use a vocabulary list for each group and check off each word as they use it. Award a prize to the group that uses the greatest number of vocabulary words.

4. Have a vocabulary treasure hunt. You can do this individually or in small groups. The idea is for the students to find and cut out as many of the vocabulary words as possible. Encourage them to search magazines, newspapers, printed advertisements, etc. They should mount each word they find on a 3" x 5" card and then write its definition. If a student finds a word in a place he or she cannot cut out (e.g., in a book or on a billboard), have him or her write the word and where he or she saw it, along with the definition, on the 3" x 5" card. The student who finds the most words wins. This is a powerful technique for making your students more aware of and alert to new vocabulary words.

5. Categorize the vocabulary words. As a whole class or in small groups, have the students sort the words into parts of speech: verb, noun, adjective, and adverb. Discuss the reason for placing words into each category (e.g., an adverb must modify a verb or adjective and usually ends in "ly").

6. Play a vocabulary bingo game. Give each student a blank bingo grid. Have students write one vocabulary word in each space on the grid. Students may place the words in any order. Then you act as the caller, randomly choosing and reading the vocabulary definitions. (Be sure you write down the words for which you've read the definitions so that you can verify a winning card.) Students place markers (beans, beads, pieces of paper, etc.) over the words that match the definitions read. A student wins by covering a row or column of words.

7. Create a mini-dictionary, using the vocabulary words. Alphabetize the words and write a definition for each one. The dictionary can be expanded to include parts of speech, sample sentences, guide words, and illustrations.

Quiz Time

Directions: Respond to the following questions in complete sentences.

1. What is the setting (time and place) of this story? _____

    _____

2. What does Kenny believe the neighbors secretly call his family? _____

    _____

3. From what you've already learned about Byron Watson, what are two of his personality traits?

    _____

    _____

4. When does Byron say, "Give my regards to Clark, Poindexter," to Kenny? _____

    _____

5. Discuss two problems that Kenny faces at school. _____

    _____

6. Do you agree with Kenny's statement that God sent Rufus to be his saver? Explain why.

    _____

    _____

7. Who is Buphead? _____

8. What causes trouble in Kenny's and Rufus's friendship? _____

    _____

9. Name two people who treat Kenny badly. What do they do to him? _____

    _____

10. Name two things that Momma does that indicate she's a caring person. _____

    _____

11. Why do you think Rufus and Cody eat a part of Kenny's lunch each day?

    _____

    _____

12. Do you think it was a good idea for Kenny to tell Byron that Larry Dunn had stolen his gloves? Explain. _____

    _____

Dinosaurs

LJ figures out a clever way to steal the majority of Kenny's toy dinosaurs. After reading the information below, pick two types of dinosaurs and fill in the Venn diagram on page 42. In the part where the circles overlap, fill in the things that the two dinosaurs have in common. In the parts that don't overlap, fill in things that apply to just that particular dinosaur.

Tyrannosaurus Rex

The Tyrannosaurus Rex is one of the most widely known and most terrifying of dinosaurs. This large, meat-eating animal lived and hunted alone. It walked upright on two legs; had sharp, jagged teeth; and had tiny "arms" with two fingers on each one. Despite its great weight, it could overtake prey by running up to 22 miles per hour (35 kpm). In addition to catching live dinosaurs, tyrannosaurus also ate the bodies of dinosaurs that died from natural causes.

Triceratops

Triceratops were plant-eating dinosaurs that lived in herds. Each triceratops had a large frill at the base of its three-horned head, a sharp beak to chop leaves from plants, and flat teeth to shred the leaves. The frill protected its neck and had blood vessels on the underside to radiate excess heat. Triceratops used its horns to defend itself against meat-eating dinosaurs.

Apatosaurus

Apatosauruses were the biggest animals ever to live on land. These plant-eating dinosaurs moved slowly in large herds. Apatosauruses had long necks, small heads, and very long tails that they used as a whip or a club to ward off attacks by meat-eating dinosaurs. Their feet had five toes with claws on the inner toes for balance. The natural life-span of an apatosaurus was about 100 years.

Learning About the Empire State Building

In chapter 1, Buphead and Byron show Kenny how to survive a blizzard by spinning him around and throwing him in the snow. Kenny has padding from the many layers of warm clothing that his mother makes him wear. Kenny quips, "These guys couldn't hurt me if they'd thrown me off the Empire State Building."

The Empire State Building is a famous landmark that has graced the New York City skyline for more than 70 years. When it was built in 1931, it was the tallest building in the world, and it enjoyed that status until 1973. Even today, the Empire State Building and its colorful history fascinate people. Your students will enjoy learning about this interesting structure.

Have students work in pairs or trios. (If necessary, the class can be broken into larger groups.)

There are two Web sites listed in the resources on page 44 that may be available; or you can ask your students to search the Web using these keywords:

- Empire State Building
- ESBNYC
- NYC tourist
- New York City landmarks

1. If your students do not have Internet access, they can use encyclopedias or the definitive reference, *The Empire State Building: The Making of a Landmark* by John Tauranac.

2. The students' goal is to locate and write down five interesting facts about the Empire State Building that they don't think anyone else in the class will choose. Here are a few examples:

   - Every year, people compete to see who can be the first to climb the building's 1,860 steps.
   - The building has 3,194,547 light bulbs.
   - The building's electrical bill tops $4.5 million annually.
   - On July 28, 1945, an Air Force B-25 crashed into the building between the 79th and 80th floors. Fourteen people were killed.
   - The only way the building could pay its taxes during the Depression was by charging visitors to go up to the observation deck.

3. Bring the class together as a whole. Have each team state their facts. They earn one point for every fact they found that no one else mentioned. (You'll be pleased at how closely they listen to each other's facts.)

4. The winning team(s) can have a prize, such as a no-homework-night pass or something else that is appropriate.

Greek Mythology

When Byron is stuck to the car mirror, it reminds Joetta of a story Kenny read to her about a man named "Nar-sissy." She is actually referring to the Greek myth of Narcissus. A myth is an old story that was once believed to be true. Greek myths first started around 3000 BC. The Greek people believed that all natural things had spirits. They also believed that some things had magical powers. Over time, their beliefs developed into legends about natural objects, animals, and gods. These gods all had human forms and emotions. Many of these legends are still well known; they are called classical Greek mythology. Read the version of the Narcissus legend below and then, using complete sentences, answer the questions that follow.

The Myth of Narcissus

Zeus, the supreme god, persuaded Echo to distract his wife, Hera, by chattering incessantly. He did this so that Hera could not keep track of Zeus, leaving him free to chase other women. However, when Hera figured out the plan, she was so enraged that she took away Echo's voice, leaving her with only the ability to repeat the final word of every message she heard. When Echo saw the extremely handsome but vain Narcissus, she fell deeply in love with him. Of course, she could not tell him of her love, but she followed him everywhere, gazing at him lovingly until he haughtily rejected her. Poor Echo hid in a cave and wasted away until only her voice remained. Then the goddess Nemesis decided to punish Narcissus by making him fall hopelessly in love with his own face as he saw it reflected in a pool. He gazed in fascination, unable to tear himself away from his image, until he gradually wasted away. In the spot where he had sat grew a beautiful yellow flower, which even to this day bears the name narcissus.

1. What did Zeus ask Echo to do? _____

_____

2. Why did he ask her to do this? _____

_____

3. What was Hera's reaction? _____

_____

4. Why did Echo fall in love with Narcissus? _____

_____

5. What was Narcissus's reaction to Echo? _____

_____

6. What did Nemesis do to Narcissus? _____

_____

7. What happened to Echo in the end? _____

_____

8. What happened to Narcissus in the end? _____

_____

Extension: Read another myth. Write a brief summary of the story on the back of this paper.

Reader's Response Journals

Writing often helps clarify thinking because it requires students to put their thoughts, feelings, and ideas into words. To build greater personal meaning and understanding of *The Watsons Go to Birmingham—1963*, have students create reader's response journals. These journals will provide them with a written record of their thoughts as they progress through the book. Requiring journals ensures that students respond to what they've read. A reader's response journal encourages the students to go back and reread passages of the novel and to reflect upon what they've read. Such reflection promotes personal involvement with the book by stimulating students to react to the characters, conflicts, actions, and events. Here are a few ideas for using reader's response journals in your classroom:

- Discuss the purpose of reader's response journals. Motivate the class by encouraging the students to use their journals as a way to express their personal feelings about the book and related issues in their own lives.

- Using passages from the book, model the journal-writing process for the class. Show students how you would record your own feelings, thoughts, ideas, observations, and questions about what you've read.

- Emphasize to the students that you are the only person besides themselves who will see the journal entries; they will not be required to share them with classmates.

- To encourage risk-taking and creative expression, be sure to explain that you will not be grading the grammar, spelling, or writing mechanics in the entries.

- Provide students with journal starters, such as these:

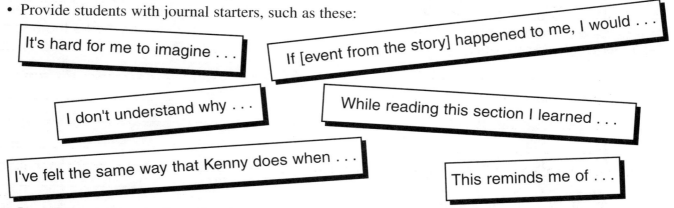

It's hard for me to imagine . . .

If [event from the story] happened to me, I would . . .

I don't understand why . . .

While reading this section I learned . . .

I've felt the same way that Kenny does when . . .

This reminds me of . . .

- Locate three passages from the chapters the class is working on. Invite your students to choose which of these passages they feel most interested in responding to and have them write their response. Here are some examples from Section 1:

"It's no wonder the neighbors called us the Weird Watsons behind our backs. There we were, all five of us standing around a car with the temperature about a million degrees below zero and each and every one of us crying!"

"The Langston Hughes book jumped from my hand and the whole class laughed, everyone but Byron. His eyes locked on mine and I felt things start melting inside of me."

"This saver stuff wasn't going anything like I thought it was supposed to. Rufus started acting like I was his friend."

- Have volunteers share their responses. Never require a student to share an entry with the class. Provide feedback to the students, gently encouraging greater clarity if necessary. Since response journals are about the students' feelings and opinions, it's crucial that you accept whatever they've written, even if you disagree.

Quiz Time

Directions: Respond to the following questions in complete sentences.

1. Who is Joetta? _____

   _____

2. Describe Byron's "Nazi Parachutes Attack America and Get Shot Down Over the Flint River" movie. _____

   _____

3. How does Joetta stop her mother from burning Byron with a match? _____

   _____

4. Why is Momma so upset about Byron playing with matches? _____

   _____

5. Why was Kenny surprised when he came across the popsicle-stick cross in the alley? _____

   _____

6. How do you think Byron felt about killing the mourning dove? Explain. _____

   _____

   _____

7. Who is Grandma Sands? _____

   _____

8. Explain what a "butter" or "conk" is and how it fits into the story. _____

   _____

   _____

9. What might have happened if Byron had run away before Dad came home and saw his "conk"?

   _____

   _____

10. Describe the similarities between Kenny and Byron. _____

    _____

    _____

11. What do all of Byron's Latest Fantastic Adventures have in common? _____

    _____

    _____

12. How do you think Byron felt about being sent to live in Alabama for the summer? Explain.

    _____

    _____

    _____

Character Sketches

One of things that makes *The Watsons Go to Birmingham—1963* so enjoyable is the characters. Often, more than any other factor, having interesting, believable characters makes a story. In fact, noted children's author Megan Whalen Turner has said that she'd change the setting or even the plot before she'd have a character do something that was out of character. This activity will help your students to understand how an author creates believable characters.

Procedure

Explain that authors often create character sketches before they ever start writing a story. This enables them to know how each character will act in a situation. Realistic characters have flaws and shortcomings. Sometimes, authors base characters on people they know or create composites of several real people. They give the person typical gestures and ways of speaking, like Kenny's habit of saying, ". . . might as well have tied him to a tree and said, 'Ready, aim, fire.'"

As a class, choose Kenny or Byron. On the board or overhead, elicit responses for each of the numbered items below. When you are done, you will have a very accurate character sketch of the boy. Review the character sketch with the class. Christopher Paul Curtis went through this process before he ever began writing the book.

Next, have your students assume a detective-type role. They will create a character sketch by closely observing (preferably secretly) a family member of their choice for two to four days. Warn them not to invade the person's privacy (by looking in their purse, pockets, dresser drawers, etc.). Each student should take careful notes about the questions below. The more description, the better the character sketch. Ask for volunteers to share their character sketches with the class.

1. Use the person's initials rather than a name or nickname. Describe the person's hair, eyes, and skin. Use a lot of adjectives to give details about each feature (e.g., large, jet-black eyes; dark, wavy hair pulled back in a ponytail; etc.).
2. What type of clothes does the person usually wear?
3. What are the person's typical gestures? typical sayings?
4. What does the person do when he or she is angry? happy? sad? stressed? excited? lonely?
5. Who does the person live with?
6. Where does the person live?
7. What does the person do well?
8. What does the person do very poorly?
9. What is the person's bedroom like?
10. What does the person enjoy doing?
11. What is the person afraid of? worried about?
12. Who is the person's friends? playmates? co-workers?
13. How does the person spend the day?
14. What does the person do to relax?
15. What is the person's job or grade in school?
16. What kinds of things does the person do that gets him or her in trouble? Who does the person get in trouble with?

Finding Sensory Images

The goal of a reader when reading might be to "make a movie" in his or her mind of what is happening. That's why well-written novels often contain a lot of sensory imagery. Sensory imagery makes it easier for the reader to envision what is happening. Sensory imagery also lets the reader experience the story more fully. In this activity your students will look for examples of sensory imagery.

Procedure

1. Discuss sensory imagery with the class. Perhaps the best way to do that is to read the following quotes from the book and ask the students which of their five senses each one appealed to.

   > "Dad was doing his best not to explode laughing. Big puffs of smoke were coming out of his nose and mouth as he tried to squeeze his laughs down. Finally, he put his head on his arms and leaned against the car's hood and howled." (*sight and hearing*)

   > "About a million fingers pointed at the new kids and a million laughs almost knocked them over." (*sight and hearing*)

   > "Byron was on take seven when Momma finally wondered why the toilet was being flushed so much and came upstairs to see what was going one. The whole upstairs smelled like a giant match . . ." (*smell*)

2. Now put the students into groups of three or four. They are to scan pages 1–120 to find one example of sensory imagery. They need to write one example for sight, one for hearing, one for taste, one for touch, and one for smell. The examples they select must be different from the ones that you read to the class.

3. When the class reconvenes, ask which sense was the easiest to find examples for (i.e., sight). Ask which sense was the hardest to find examples for (i.e., taste or smell).

4. Ask each group to read one of their five examples aloud and tell which sense the example appealed to.

sight   sound   smell   taste   touch

Music Critiques

In this part of the book, the Watsons get the Ultra-Glide, and we readers start to find out about the kinds of music they enjoy listening to. The "oldies" with asterisks are mentioned by name in the book. The others are readily available songs by the artists that Kenny mentions his parents playing on the Ultra-Glide.

★ "Yakety Yak" by the Coasters (Kenny's favorite)*

★ "Under the Boardwalk" by the Drifters (Momma's favorite)*

★ "Straighten Up and Fly Right" by Nat King Cole (Dad likes to whistle this)*

★ "Unforgettable" by Nat King Cole

★ "I've Got You Under My Skin" by Dinah Washington

★ "What a Difference a Day Makes" by Dinah Washington

★ "Smoke Gets In Your Eyes" by Dinah Washington

1. Obtain a copy of these songs on cassette or CD. You may even be able to access them on the Web. Play each one for the class.

2. If possible, read the students one or two music critiques from a magazine such as *Teen People*, *Spin*, or *Teen*. Post these phrases (which were taken from various music critiques in *Rolling Stone*):

   • "hokey, save-the-world lyrics"   • "bounces along on a perky melody"

   • "intensely rhythmic"   • "they harmonize well"

   • "too dull; sleep-inducing"   • "sassiest rock-and-roll rhythms"

   • "likable, danceable beat"   • "plunges listeners into"

   • "singing sounds a little tired"

3. Put the students into teams of three. Assign each group a different song or artist from the list above. Each group may listen to their song several times. Then they discuss and formulate answers to these questions:

   • What do you like about the song?

   • What did the recording artist do especially well?

   • What do you dislike about the song?

   • What could the recording artist have done better?

   • How is this song different from the songs of today?

   • How is this song like the songs of today?

   • What age group do you think this song appeals to (children, teens, adults, senior citizens)?

   • Would you recommend that another person your age buy this song?

4. Have each team use their answers to prepare a music critique for a teen magazine. Encourage them to use one or more of the phrases that you posted.

Creating Portmanteau Words

Skillful authors sometimes make new words when they feel there is no appropriate word in our language for what they want to say. These words are called portmanteau words. Portmanteau means combining two words to create a new word. Sometimes portmanteau words become a part of our language. Two portmanteau words you might already know are:

- *chortle* (a combination of "chuckle" and "snort")

- *scurrying* (a combination of "hurrying" and "scrambling")

Directions: Christopher Paul Curtis introduced several portmanteau words in *The Watsons Go to Birmingham—1963*. Read these quotes. Highlight (or underline) the portmanteau word in each. On the lines provided, write the two words you believe the author combined.

_____ + _____   1. "He noticed that when I talked to people I squinched my lazy eye kind of shut or that I'd put my hand on my face to cover it."

_____ + _____   2. "'Now all of you will help Rufus feel welcome, won't you?' Someone sniggled."

_____ + _____   3. "The toilet stopped glugging . . ."

_____ + _____   4. "You really gonna make me go embarrass myself by signing a welfare list for some groceries like a blanged peon?"

Extension: Now that you understand the concept, trying creating two portmanteau words yourself. Use your portmanteau words in a sentence so the reader has a context to understand the word. Challenge your classmates or teacher to figure out the two words you combined.

1. _____

_____

2. _____

_____

Quiz Time

Directions: Respond to the following questions in complete sentences.

1. What is the Ultra-Glide? _____

2. What does Dad tell Kenny is the reason that Byron is being sent to Birmingham?

   _____

   _____

3. Name three things that Momma did to get ready for the trip to Birmingham._____

   _____

   _____

4. Why do you think Mrs. Davidson gave Joetta the angel statue? _____

   _____

5. Did you think that Byron was going to make the entire trip without speaking? _____

   _____

6. Of the places that the Watsons stop during their trip, which one would have interested you the most? Explain why._____

   _____

   _____

   _____

7. Name two things that frightened both Kenny and Byron at the two different rest stops.

   _____

   _____

8. Why doesn't anyone want to hold Joey's head while she sleeps? _____

   _____

9. How would the Watsons' trip have been different if they had followed Momma's plan?

   _____

   _____

10. How does Grandma Sands compare to Kenny's expectations?_____

    _____

11. Why do you think that Momma seems so upset about Mr. Robert?_____

    _____

12. Who do you think will triumph this summer: Byron or Grandma Sands? Explain.

    _____

    _____

    _____

Recreate the Brown Bomber

Directions: Kenny gives a vivid description of the Brown Bomber. Using this information and your imagination, recreate the Brown Bomber in one of the following ways:

❏ Using watercolors, pastels, or markers, do a detailed painting or drawing of the Brown Bomber.

❏ Create a computer 3-D model of the Brown Bomber using graphics software.

❏ Build the Brown Bomber using cardboard, craft sticks, papiér-mâiché over wire frame, modeling clay, Legos™, or any other appropriate building material.

You can add any details you'd like, but you must include these four details in your drawing or model:

- the damaged hood ornament

- the Ultra-Glide

- the rearview mirror to which Byron's lips were stuck

- the bar down the front of the windshield

Tips for models

1. A wooden board will support the model's weight better than a cardboard one.

2. Use aluminum foil for chrome on the car (bumpers, hood ornament).

3. To provide a realistic setting, paint or use marker to make a road underneath the Brown Bomber; you can even glue real crushed gravel (if available).

4. Use modeling clay to create Momma, Dad, Byron, Kenny, and Joetta and place them around or inside the Brown Bomber.

5. Think of special touches you can add—for example, glue fabric on the seats for upholstery, or fashion tiny ice scrapers and glue them on the hood.

Creating Cartoon Strips

Form small groups of no more than three people. Each group will create three cartoon strips about adventures that Kenny, Byron, and Joetta have had or will have. These cartoons must be about events that weren't included in the book.

Materials Needed for Each Group

- markers or colored pencils
- Cartoon Strip Template (page 41)

Procedure

We often ask students to work in cooperative groups and expect them to know how to do so effectively. However, students often do not know how to get organized and function as a team. Following these steps will help promote group success:

1. Have students choose specific roles for each group member—leader, facilitator, and scribe.

2. Model brainstorming for the class. Be sure that they understand that all ideas, no matter how wacky, should be recorded, as they may spark better suggestions.

3. Give the group a defined amount of class time to meet. Toward the end of the meeting time (e.g., five minutes before time's up), have the students in each group set up a mutually agreeable date, time, and place to complete their teamwork (if necessary).

4. Explain to them how to use their time. For example, if you give them 30 minutes of time and they need to do three cartoon strips, after ten minutes they must drop the first cartoon and start work on the second. Set a timer and remind them. Do this again after 20 minutes. In this way, a group won't be discouraged by having spent the entire time on one cartoon without having even considered the other two.

5. Give them several methods for generating the cartoon ideas:

   - whole-group brainstorming

   - relay writing (one person writes the first scene, another does the second, the last person does the third, then hands it back to the first person to do the fourth, and so on). This method can help prevent writer's block.

   - assembly-line writing (one person completes the first one or two panels of all three cartoons, another person completes the middle one or two panels of all the cartoons, and the last person finishes the final one or two panels of all the cartoons). This method is especially effective if the group contains people who are great at thinking up openings or punchlines.

   - two people do the writing, another does the drawing

6. Use the blank cartoon-strip template on page 41.

7. Post the cartoons where they can be enjoyed—for example on a bulletin board or in the hallway.

Extension: Challenge students to use two vocabulary words in each cartoon strip.

Figurative Language

Talented writers such as Christopher Paul Curtis use figurative language to make scenes more vivid. In *The Watsons Go to Birmingham—1963* he uses these figurative language devices:

Hyperbole—an obvious exaggeration

Example: The garbage can was **the size of the Titanic**.

Simile—a comparison using the words "like" or "as"

Examples: The hungry boy ate **like a horse**. The soup was **as cold as ice**.

Metaphor—an implied comparison in which one thing is called another

Example: The girl **was a scared rabbit**.

Personification—giving human characteristics to a thing (plant, animal, or thing)

Example: The vine **clutched** at her leg and **refused** to let go.

Directions: Read each quote from the book. Decide whether it is an example of **hyperbole (H)**, **simile (S)**, **metaphor (M)**, or **personification (P)**, and write the abbreviation for your choice on the line provided. Then highlight (or underline) the words that indicated to you the type of figurative language being used. (In the examples above, these words have been bolded.)

_____ 1. "That snake in the grass has got his phone off the hook."

_____ 2. "With Byron walking around me like that we must have looked like we were in the Wild West and I was a wagon train and Byron was the Indians circling, waiting to attack."

_____ 3. "The door jumped out of her way . . ."

_____ 4. "Larry Dunn was the king of the kindergarten to fourth grade of Clark Elementary . . . but Byron was a god."

_____ 5. "Momma's voice got strange, hissing like a snake . . ."

_____ 6. "Momma said that last part like she was dropping a bomb on Grandma Sands."

_____ 7. "I knew this was a worm with a hook on it, but I bit anyway."

_____ 8. "I've got about a million [dinosaurs], but before LJ started coming over I had two million."

_____ 9. "If there was a forest fire somewhere all Smokey the Bear would have to do is hold me upside down over it and the fire wouldn't have a chance."

_____ 10. "All the kids were looking at me like I was a six-legged dog."

_____ 11. ". . . when his fingers found out it was them that were going to get burned, they let go of Byron's throat and joined the rest of his body in deciding to wait at Buphead's until Dad got home."

_____ 12. "Then he dropped the bomb on me."

Using a Road Atlas

One of the reference materials you will use repeatedly throughout your life is a road atlas. Whenever you go on a road trip, you can refer to this book of maps to find out how to get where you're going (and back again!).

1. Find a map showing the entire continental U.S. in a road atlas. Using your finger, follow the Watsons' route down I–75 from Flint, Michigan, to Birmingham, Alabama.

2. Cities appear in large bold print on a map. Refer to the road atlas to find the name of five cities that they must have passed through on their way and write them here: _____

   _____

   _____

3. Name the six states that the Watsons traveled through. Also name the capital of each of these states. Each capital's name will be shown next to a star inside a circle. _____

   _____

   _____

   _____

4. Did the Watsons travel through any of these state capitals? If so, which one(s)? _____

   _____

5. Shortly before the border of Alabama, the Watsons stopped following Route 75 and traveled on what route number? _____

6. Turn to the page showing the state of Alabama. Do any cities have their own map insets on this page? What are their names? Why do you think they have map insets? _____

   _____

   _____

   _____

7. Describe a different route (using route numbers and where they change) that the Watsons could have taken on their way back to Flint._____

   _____

   _____

Quiz Time

Directions: Respond to the following questions in complete sentences.

1. Who is Mr. Robert? _____

_____

2. What does Mr. Robert say he did for Toddy that impressed Kenny and Byron? _____

_____

_____

3. How does the Birmingham weather affect the Watson children's choice of activities? _____

_____

_____

4. Why does Grandma Sands warn the kids to stay away from Collier's Landing? _____

_____

_____

5. Why do you think Kenny defied everyone and went to Collier's Landing? _____

_____

_____

6. What caused Momma to act like a little kid that just got yelled at? _____

_____

7. What is out in the deep water that Kenny wants to catch, and why does he want it? _____

_____

_____

8. What did Grandma Sands really mean when she said there was a Wool Pooh? _____

_____

9. Describe Kenny's encounter with the Wool Pooh. _____

_____

_____

10. What would probably have happened if Byron hadn't pulled Kenny out of the water? _____

_____

11. Why do you think Kenny had a vision of Joetta in an angel costume while he was in the water?

_____

12. What do you think will happen if Kenny explains his "adventure" to his family? Explain.

_____

_____

Jackdaws

A jackdaw is an unusual bird that collects just about anything it can carry and keeps it in its nest. A jackdaw is sort of a flying version of the packrat! As an educational activity, a jackdaw is a collection of things related to a specific topic. Jackdaws have received attention as an instructional tool because they promote higher-level thinking skills in students in an enjoyable way. In addition, jackdaws look terrific in showcases or on display for parents' night or open house. They create a lot of interest throughout the school and visitors from the community.

Materials: Each student needs a large shoebox (or another large cardboard box).

Procedure

1. Each student will create a jackdaw containing at least five items to remind Kenny of 1963. Each item must include a card stating why the student chose that item.

2. Each student presents one item from his or her jackdaw to the class. They may read the card they prepared. They should strive to show an item that no one else has already presented.

3. Share these ideas only if a student is absolutely stumped:

   ◆ an old sneaker with a hole in the sole patched with a piece of cardboard

   ◆ a U.S. road map with the route from Flint to Birmingham marked in highlighter

   ◆ a notebook with the words "The Watsons Go to Birmingham—1963" and a bee trying to land on a flower drawn on the front cover

   ◆ old, brown, miniature car

   ◆ Swedish creme cookie

   ◆ packet of grape Kool Aid™

   ◆ leather gloves with fur lining

   ◆ miniature plastic dinosaur

   ◆ 45-rpm record

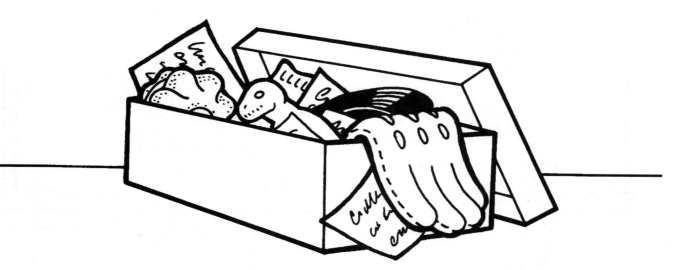

Creative Review Questions Activity

Here is an interesting and fun way for your students to quickly review the novel.

Materials

- 26 sheets of blank paper
- 13 markers

Procedure

1. Assign one chapter (from chapters 1–13) to each of 13 students.

2. Give the students about six minutes to briefly review (skim) their sections. The students who are not assigned chapters are skimming the entire book.

3. Hand out a pen and two sheets of blank paper to each student who has been assigned a chapter.

4. Each of these students writes a question based on the material in their assigned section on one of the two sheets of paper.

5. The student then writes the answer to that same question on the second sheet of paper.

6. Collect the questions in one stack and the answers in another.

7. Shuffle each stack and give every student in the class one question or one answer.

8. The students with questions stand on the left side of the room; the students with answers stand on the right side of the room.

9. Have all the students hold up the paper with the question or answer.

10. The students read the questions or answers on each other's papers and locate the person with whom they belong.

11. The answer person goes to stand with the question person.

12. Call each pair up to the front of the room. Have them stand so that the question and answer are both showing. The one with the question asks the question; the other one answers it.

13. If necessary, lead a discussion for clarification or to help the class review the information.

Learning About Weather

As in our own lives, the weather plays a part in *The Watsons Go to Birmingham—1963*. In the beginning Momma is disgusted with the cold winters in Flint, Michigan. Toward the end Kenny complains about being unable to sleep in the sticky heat of summer in Birmingham, Alabama.

Find the answers to the questions below by studying the climates in Flint, Michigan (Genesee County), and Birmingham, Alabama (Jefferson County), using traditional reference materials, CD-ROM encyclopedias, or the Internet. There are two addresses available on Resources (page 43–44). If these sites are unavailable, search using these key words:

- Northeast Regional Climate Center
- climatic data for the United States
- National Weather Service
- Regional Climate Center
- climate data

1. What are typical winter (December–March) conditions in Flint, Michigan? _____ _____

2. What's the average temperature during the winter? _____ _____

3. What's the average relative humidity during the winter? _____ _____

4. How much total snowfall usually occurs during the winter?_____ _____

5. What are the dangers associated with winter weather in Flint, Michigan? _____ _____

6. How does a Flint, Michigan, winter compare to winter where you live? _____ _____

7. What are the typical summer (June–August) conditions in Birmingham, Alabama? _____

8. What's the average temperature during the summer?_____ _____

9. What's the average relative humidity during the summer? _____ _____

10. How much total precipitation usually occurs during the summer?_____ _____

11. What are the dangers associated with summer weather in Birmingham, Alabama? _____ _____

12. How does a Birmingham, Alabama, summer compare to summer where you live? _____ _____

Doing Library Research

Library skills have taken on greater importance today than ever before. The World Wide Web has given us access to a previously unimaginable amount of information, and the ability to locate this information is one of the essential skills of the 21st century. Have students choose one of the following people or topics for research:

Topics	References Sources
• Thurgood Marshall • Ralph Abernathy • Fannie Lou Hammer • Martin Luther King, Jr. • 15th Amendment to the Constitution • Voting Rights Act (1965) • John Lewis • Medgar Evers • Rosa Parks • Mohandas Gandhi • Fair Housing Act (1968)	• encyclopedia (bound, CD, or online) • catalog of library holdings 　(online or card catalog) • dictionary • Guinness World Book of Records • microfilm/microfiche • Reader's Guide to Periodical Literature 　(bound or online) • almanac • atlas • thesaurus • Internet

As a class, present the questions below, asking students to identify the reference source(s) that would mostly likely provide the answer:

1. What reference could you use to find out how far is it from Flint, Michigan, to Birmingham, Alabama?

2. What reference could you use to find articles that have been written about the Civil Rights movement in the last five years?

3. What reference could you use to read a newspaper article from September 16, 1963?

4. What reference could you use to locate a detailed map of downtown Flint, Michigan?

5. What reference could you use to determine the longest protest boycott of the 1960s?

6. During your research you encounter the word *sanguine* and want to know its meaning. What reference would you use?

7. What reference could you use to find out what books your library has on Martin Luther King, Jr.?

8. What reference could you use to find out today's weather in Flint, Michigan?

9. You want a synonym for the word *discrimination* so that you won't have to say the same word repeatedly during your talk. What reference would you use?

10. What reference could you use to find a general overview of the Civil Rights movement?

When you have covered all the materials and their usage, allow students time in the library to research their topic. Students should prepare a three-minute talk about what they discovered. They can present their speech to the class or speak it into a tape recorder (for you to review at a convenient time). Students must submit a list of the reference materials they used. This can just be a list of titles and doesn't need to be written in bibliographical format.

Quiz Time

Directions: Respond to the following questions in complete sentences.

1. Does Kenny tell his parents about his near drowning? Tell why or why not. _____

    _____

2. What does Kenny say to Joey as she leaves for Sunday school? _____

    _____

3. What does Kenny do when he reaches the church? _____

    _____

4. What causes Kenny to flee from the church? _____

    _____

5. Back at Grandma Sands's house, why doesn't Kenny want to look at Joetta? _____

    _____

6. Since Kenny wasn't physically there, who or what do you think lured Joetta from the church?

    _____

    _____

7. Where is the World-Famous Watson Pet Hospital, and who goes to hide there? _____

    _____

    _____

8. What did Byron do to lure Kenny from behind the couch? Name at least three things. _____

    _____

    _____

    _____

9. What does Kenny tell Byron he feels ashamed about? _____

    _____

10. What is Byron's opinion of the Wool Pooh, magic powers, and genies? Explain. _____

    _____

    _____

11. What does the Wool Pooh symbolize to Kenny? Explain. _____

    _____

    _____

12. Does this story seem believable to you? Give at least two reasons that support your answer.

    _____

    _____

    _____

Portraying Major Events in Each Character's Life

In most good books, as in life, the characters grow and change; they do not remain static. Events happen to them that make them see, do, and think about things differently.

Materials

- at least five sheets of drawing paper for each student and a drawing medium (markers, pastels, colored pencils), or access to computers with drawing software

Have students draw a portrait depicting how they envision each of the main characters in the book: Kenny, Byron, Joetta, Momma, and Dad. Next, they should decide on the four main events that happened to each person. They will write each of these events on the different corners of the appropriate portrait, as shown below. These corners should be folded down so that there's no peeking until everyone is done.

When students are finished, have them compare their work with that of the rest of the class. Lead a class discussion based on these questions: Did everyone choose the same four events? Why might some be different?

Literature Circles

Discuss with the class that great authors often use symbolism to explore complex ideas. In *The Watsons Go to Birmingham—1963* Kenny uses the Wool Pooh to describe evil, terror, and death.

The following activity will help make students aware of literary symbolism. Students' own creative writing pieces will be strengthened if you encourage them to use symbolism to help make a point or to engage their readers.

Materials

- construction paper or poster board
- marking pens
- student copies of a short story that employs symbolism. Not all literature circles must read the same short story; in fact, it makes the activity more interesting if they don't. Here are some suggestions:
    - ❑ "The Legend of Pin Oak," "Justice," or "The Woman in the Snow," all in Patricia C. McKissack's *The Dark Thirty*, a Newbery honor book of African-American short stories from the South
    - ❑ "The Tell-Tale Heart" by Edgar Allan Poe*
    - ❑ "The Grave" by Katherine Anne Porter
    - ❑ "The Monkey's Paw" by W. W. Jacobs
    - ❑ "The Last Leaf" by O. Henry
    - ❑ "The Adventure of the Speckled Band" by Sir Arthur Conan Doyle**

Directions

1. With the entire class, read and discuss the passages about the Wool Pooh in *The Watsons Go to Birmingham—1963*.
    - ❑ How does the Wool Pooh make you feel?
    - ❑ What was Curtis trying to say when he described the Wool Pooh as faceless?
    - ❑ What was the significance of the gray coloring? the square toes? the square fingers?
    - ❑ Was it essential that Kenny met the Wool Pooh twice? Why?
2. Divide the class into literature circles of four. Have students read the assigned short story for homework. Then, each literature circle should discuss the symbolism in the short story.
3. Next the group members should compare and contrast the symbolism in the short story to the symbolism of the Wool Pooh.
4. On the construction paper, the students should make a two-column chart with these headings: *similarities* and *differences*. Each group must list at least two similarities and two differences.
5. When this activity is done, reconvene as a whole group. Select a group member from each literature circle to share the group's chart.
6. Conclude with a class discussion of the following points:
    - ❑ Why do authors use symbolism?
    - ❑ When do authors use symbolism?
    - ❑ How does symbolism engage a reader's interest?
    - ❑ What do you like about symbolism?
    - ❑ What do you dislike about symbolism?
    - ❑ Must symbolism have significance to the rest of the story? In what way?

*May be available to download for free from *www.literature.org*. **May be available to download for free from *www.bragi.com*.

Math Problems

Directions: Find the answers to the following questions.* Be sure to show your work and include a label with your answers.

1. Byron's birthday is January 16, 1950; Kenny's birthday is February 4, 1953; and Joetta's birthday is May 1, 1958. How much older is Byron than Kenny in years, months, and days?

2. How much older is Kenny than Joetta in years, months, and days?

3. The Watsons started for Birmingham with 30 gallons of gas in their tank. When they stopped for gas, they had to buy 29 gallons to refill the tank. They had driven 375 miles. Find how many miles per gallon the Brown Bomber used from Flint, Michigan, to Cincinnati, Ohio, to the nearest tenth of a gallon.

4. To travel from Flint to Birmingham took 26 hours. Joetta slept for 18 hours, Kenny slept for 16 ½ hours, Byron slept for 15 hours, and Momma slept for 13 hours. Find the percentage of the total trip time each person spent asleep to the nearest whole percent.

5. The damage caused to the church by the bombing was $458,000. Insurance covered only $250,000. To raise the remaining funds, the church held a baked goods sale that earned $9,000 and a rummage sale that earned $26,000. Private donations to repair the church reached $92,000. What was the amount of the loan that the congregation had to get to repair the church?

*All dates and figures are fictitious.

Compare Yourself to Kenny or Byron

Reading literature helps us gain insight into life by letting us explore life through its characters. The more an author can get us to empathize and relate to a character, the more we feel connected and interested in the book. In addition, through the exploration of a character's change and growth, we often learn more about ourselves.

Directions: Choose to compare yourself to either Kenny or Byron. Think about the prompts below and how you would answer them for your chosen character. Next, think about the prompts below and how you would answer them for yourself. Then complete a Venn diagram. (Use the blank template provided on page 42.) In the left circle, write things that apply only to the character. In the right circle, write things that apply only to you. In the middle section, write things that apply to both of you. You do not need to use the prompts given, and you can add any other things you'd like.

❑ family size	❑ parents
❑ pastimes	❑ likes
❑ teased	❑ abilities
❑ grandma	❑ adventurous
❑ birth order	❑ streetwise
❑ feelings about siblings	❑ confident
❑ trying to be "cool"	❑ dislikes
❑ sense of humor	❑ bully
❑ types of friends	❑ caring
❑ appearance	❑ embarrassed
❑ fears	❑ defiant
❑ swearing	❑ needs
❑ problems	

Extension: When you have finished, write a three-paragraph summary based on the Venn diagram. In the first paragraph, describe how you are like the character you chose. In the second paragraph, describe how you are different from the character. In the third paragraph, conclude by stating whether you are more similar to or different from the character.

Book Report Ideas

There are many ways to report on a book once you have read it. After you have completed *The Watsons Go to Birmingham—1963*, have each student choose one method of reporting on the book, using the ideas given here or others you or the students devise.

Book Character

Choose a character from the book (Byron, Kenny, Joetta, Momma, Dad, Buphead, or Rufus) and dress up like the character. Tell the class the story from your character's perspective.

Board Game

Student partners can create a board game based on the events in the story. Be sure to include instructions for play, use of the game board, and all the necessary game pieces.

Into the Future

Write a chapter of what happens next, now that Kenny has come out from behind the couch.

News Interview

A pair of students performs this book report in Barbara Walters's style. One student pretends to be Kenny, Byron, or Joetta, completely immersed in the character. The other student plays the role of a television or newspaper reporter, reporting on the church bombing in Birmingham and trying to provide the audience with insights into the character's personality and life. It can be fun but challenging for the partners to create a realistic, meaningful dialogue.

Critique

Write a brief, specific opinion statement about *The Watsons Go to Birmingham—1963* (for example, "I would recommend this book to a friend because I enjoyed reading about Kenny's experiences growing up in the early 1960s," or "I disliked this book because I prefer action-packed adventure stories."). Use several examples to back up your opinion. "It was neat" is not sufficient. Share your critique with the class.

Annotation

Although it sounds simple, it is actually quite a challenging task for students: sum up the plot in one sentence without giving the ending away. All American books have a Library of Congress annotation written for them by a trained professional (for example, "A 10-year-old African-American boy details his adventures as a middle child in the early 1960s, including his first confrontation with the evil of racism.").

Dramatization

Have students work in small groups to select and act out one scene from the book. The group can decide to include costumes and props for greater effect. The group then presents the scene for the class or another class in order to promote the book. At the close of the dramatization, one of the students explains the significance of the scene to the whole book.

The Newbery Medal

In 1922 the American Library Association Executive Board established the Newbery Medal in order to "encourage original creative work in the field of books for children." The Newbery is named after John Newbery, an 18th-centruy bookseller, and is awarded anually. Each year, at least one other book is also recognized as a Newbery Medal Honor Book. In 1996 Christopher Paul Curtis's *The Watsons Go to Birmingham—1963* was named a Newbery Medal Honor Book, and in 2000 his second novel, *Bud, Not Buddy*, was awarded the top prize: the Newbery Medal.

Directions: In short essay form, answer the following questions about Newbery Medals and *The Watsons Go to Birmingham—1963*. For reference, the Newbery Medal's official Web site can be accessed by using a search engine and typing in the key word "Newbery."

> ## The Newbery Medal Goes to . . .
>
> *A Year Down Yonder* (2001)
> —Richard Peck
>
> *Holes* (1999)
> —Louis Sachar
>
> *Roll of Thunder, Hear My Cry* (1977)
> —Mildred D. Taylor
>
> *A Wrinkle in Time* (1963)
> —Madeleine L'Engle
>
> *The Twenty-One Balloons* (1948)
> —William Péne Du Bois

❑ In 1996 *The Watsons Go to Birmingham—1963* was named a Newbery Medal Honor Book. Do you think it deserved this honor? Why or why not? Support your argument with specific examples from the book.

_____

_____

_____

_____

❑ Have you read any other Newbery Medal-winning novels? If so, which ones? If not, are there any books that you've read that you feel should have won the Newbery Medal but didn't? Give the title and author's name of at least one book and provide support statements for your argument

_____

_____

_____

_____

Culminating Activities

You can select or allow students to choose one of the following culminating activities to demonstrate the knowledge they acquired as a result of reading *The Watsons Go to Birmingham—1963*:

Small Group Activities

1. For 14 years the bombing of the Sixteenth Street Baptist Church went unsolved. Then, in 1977, long-time Ku Klux Klan member Robert Chambliss was convicted of the crime. However, authorities always suspected others were involved. Finally, on May 1, 2001, Thomas Blanton Jr. was also convicted and sentenced to four consecutive life terms. At the time of this printing, Bobby Frank Cherry was awaiting trial for his alleged participation.

   Form a small group of no more than three people. Research the church bombing that took place in 1963 in Birmingham, Alabama. Create a multimedia presentation (*PowerPoint* slide show, poster, or song) to share the information you learned with the class.

2. Form a small group of no more than four people. Write a skit about an adventure that Kenny, Bryon, and Joetta have that is not included in the book. There must be a speaking part for each person in the group. You will perform your skit for the class.

Individual Activities

1. Research cars of the 1960s and those of today to find their similarities and differences. Create a poster or chart to share the information you learn.

2. Create a comic book depicting at least four of the funny scenes from the book (e.g., when Byron got his lips frozen to the car mirror; when Byron tells Joetta and Kenny about the garbage trucks picking up the Southern people who had frozen dead in their tracks, etc.).

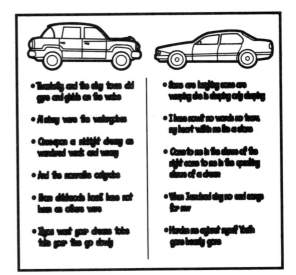

Unit Test

Part I: Matching (4 points each)

Directions: Match the word to their synonyms. Not all choices are used.

_____ 1. emulate   A. provoke

_____ 2. hypnotize   B. intrude

_____ 3. peon   C. mesmerize

_____ 4. cussing   D. separation

_____ 5. maestro   E. peasant

_____ 6. accustomed   F. used to

_____ 7. pathetic   G. imitate

_____ 8. trespass   H. widespread

_____ 9. pervasive   I. passionate

_____10. segregation   J. master

                                     K. pitiable

                                     L. swearing

Part II: True/False/Explain (4 points each)

Directions: Number a sheet of paper 1–15, leaving at least two lines between each. Read each statement. Write **True** or **False** on the paper. If the answer is false, you must explain why it is false (or what would make it true). You must include *both parts* to receive any credit for a **False** answer.

Example: At Clark Elementary School, Larry Dunn was more important than Byron.

Answer: False. Kenny says that Larry Dunn is the "king" of the kindergarten to grade 4, but Byron is a "god."

1. Byron is angry when Kenny reads in front of his class.

2. When Byron skips school, he says to Kenny, "Give my regards to Clark, Poindexter."

3. Cody is Kenny's saver.

4. Byron tells Kenny and Joetta that people with Southern blood freeze dead in their tracks in Flint.

5. Momma helps repair Kenny's and Rufus's relationship.

6. Byron is delighted when he throws a cookie at a mourning dove and kills it.

7. Dad gives Byron a conk.

8. Grandma Sands agrees to let Byron live with her for the summer.

9. Joey likes the angel Mrs. Davidson gives to her.

10. Byron sleeps on his parents' floor the night before the trip to Birmingham.

11. Dad ruins Momma's plans by driving straight through to Birmingham.

12. When he's in the water, Kenny escapes from the Wool Pooh by himself.

13. Joey is injured in the church bombing.

14. After the bombing, the Watsons don't let Byron stay in Birmingham for the rest of the summer.

15. Byron refuses to help Kenny out of his depression.

Quotations

Directions: Choose 10 of the following quotes. Reread each one in the book so you know the context. Then thoroughly explain the meaning of each one on a separate sheet of paper. Be sure to include the question number.

1. *Chapter 2:* "Mr. Alums might as well have tied me to a pole and said, 'Ready, aim, fire!'"

2. *Chapter 3:* "LJ finally pulled the trick I knew he was going to but he did it so cool that I didn't even see it coming."

3. *Chapter 4:* "Byron was the only person who could make you feel sorry for someone as mean as Larry Dunn."

4. *Chapter 4:* "I couldn't stand to see how the movie was going to end, so me and Rufus left."

5. *Chapter 6:* "Leave it to Daddy Cool to torture human kids at school all day long and never have his conscience bother him but to feel sorry for a stupid little grayish brown bird."

6. *Chapter 7:* "'You think I'm hurt and you and every other punk Chihuahua in America is climbing out of the woodwork to try and get a bite out of me.'"

7. *Chapter 8:* "It's times like this when someone is talking to you like you are a grown-up that you have to be careful not to pick your nose or dig your drawers out of your butt."

8. *Chapter 10:* "Having a little pee in your pants had to be better than being dinner for some redneck."

9. *Chapter 12:* "I'd never seen Momma act like a little kid who just got yelled at but there she was, picking at a piece of paper towel and looking kind of embarrassed."

10. *Chapter 13:* "Byron was shaking like he was getting electrocuted and crying like a baby and kissing the top of my head over and over!"

11. *Chapter 14:* "The light flickered and the smoke cleared, and I could see that hanging on to the other end of the shoe was a giant gray hand with cold, hard square fingers."

12. *Chapter 15:* "I was waiting to see if the magic powers were going to treat me like a dog or a cat, or if when Byron or Joey woke up one morning they'd find a crumpled-up yellow towel where I was supposed to be."

13. *Chapter 15:* "If he'd ever had his ankle grabbed by it, he'd know it was real, if he'd seen the way it was crouched down, crawling around in the dust and the smoke of the church in Birmingham, he'd know it wasn't some made-up garbage, if he'd ever seen those horrible toes, he'd know the Wool Pooh was as serious as a heart attack."

14. *Chapter 15:* "And I'm sure there was an angel in Birmingham when Grandma Sands wrapped her little arms around all of the Weird Watsons and said, 'My fambly, my beautiful, beautiful fambly.'"

Conversations

Choose five of the following situations. Work with a partner to write the conversations that might have occurred in each situation. Each conversation should be at least six sentences long. Be sure to write the number of each conversation.

1. Kenny tells Momma about Rufus and Cody sharing his peanut butter sandwiches and apples.

2. Byron confronts LJ and demands that he return Kenny's dinosaurs.

3. Kenny explains to Rufus why he laughed at Cody after he checked his pants during the bus ride to school.

4. Byron discusses getting a conk with Buphead.

5. Byron explains to his parents why he bought Swedish cremes on their grocery account.

6. Joetta explains to Kenny and Byron why she dislikes the angel Mrs. Davidson gave to her.

7. Dad confronts Byron about playing with matches in the bathroom.

8. Kenny describes the Wool Pooh to Rufus.

9. Joetta tells her parents what happened to Kenny and Byron at the whirlpool.

10. Kenny explains to Rufus what happened in Birmingham.

11. A Birmingham resident who saw Kenny leave the church carrying the black shoe calls a newspaper reporter to tell what he or she has seen.

12. Byron tells Kenny how he feels about what happened at the whirlpool.

13. Byron explains to his parents why Kenny is staying behind the couch.

14. Kenny's parents discuss what they should do about Byron since he didn't spend the summer with Grandma Sands.

15. Momma tells Kenny why she's upset about Grandma Sands and Mr. Robert.

Cartoon Strip Template

Use the template below to complete the activity on page 22.

Venn Diagram Template

Use the template below to complete the activities on pages 11 and 34.

Bibliography of Related Readings

Civil Rights Movement Fiction

Armistead, John. *The $66 Summer*. Milkweed Editions, 2000. In 1955 Alabama small-town racism and bigotry surface when 12-year-old black and white boys try to solve a mystery together.

Johnson, Angela. *Toning the Sweep*. Orchard Books, 1991. Set in the present, this award-winning book shows how a 14-year-old girl comes to understand history through the stories of her mother and grandmother, whose husband was lynched in Alabama in 1964.

Sebestyen, Ouida. *Words by Heart*. Yearling Books, 1997. A 12-year-old African-American girl learns to forgive and not nurture hatred when her winning a Bible-quoting contest causes violence, and her beloved father is killed.

Civil Rights Movement Nonfiction

Bridges, Ruby. *Through My Eyes*. Scholastic, 1999. Ruby Bridges recounts her experiences as the first grader who needed federal escorts to integrate an all-white school in New Orleans in 1961.

Engelbert, Phillis. *American Civil Rights: Primary Sources*. UKL, 1999. Presents 15 historically significant documents, including speeches, autobiographical text, and proclamations. Of particular interest: Dr. Martin Luther King's "I Have a Dream" speech and his famous "Letter from Birmingham Jail."

Harding, Vincent and Robin Kelley and Earl Lewis. *We Changed the World: African Americans, 1945–1970*. Oxford University Press, 1997. This book is written for grades 9 and up, but the photographs will be of interest.

King, Casey and Linda Barrett Osbourne. *Oh, Freedom! Kids Talk About the Civil Rights Movements With the People Who Made It Happen*. Knopf, 1997. Children interview adults about their civil-rights experiences, helping the reader to understand what it was like to be an African American in the 1960s. Includes historical articles to provide background.

Lee, Spike. *Four Little Girls*. HBO Home Video, 1999 (VHS video), 2000 (DVD). This 102-minute documentary chronicles the events leading up to the 1963 Birmingham church bombing, sensitively portrays the horror of that fateful day, and examines the repercussions.

Levine, Ellen. *Freedom's Children: Young Civil Rights Activists Tell Their Own Stories*. Puffin, 2000. People recount their Civil Rights memories, allowing the reader to see what it was like to be an African-American child in the South during the 1960s.

Lucas, Eileen. *Civil Rights: The Long Struggle*. Enslow Publishers, Inc., 1996. Details the progress of the African-American fight for racial justice and equality in an interesting, readable format.

Myers, Walter Dean. *Now Is Your Time: The African American Struggle for Freedom*. HarperCollins, 1992. This award-winning book provides an in-depth look at the African-American experience from slavery through the Civil Rights era.

Patterson, Charles. *The Civil Rights Movement*. Facts-on-File, 1995. This title, part of the Social Reform Movement series, details the African-American struggle for equality and the significance of the Civil Rights movement in American history.

Vernell, Marjorie. *Leaders of Black Civil Rights*. Lucent Books, 2000. A collection of biographies of important African-American leaders.

Weatherford, Carole Boston. *The African-American Struggle for Legal Equality in American History*. Written specifically for middle school students, this book includes source documents.

Bibliography of Related Readings *(cont.)*

Greek Mythology

Blaisdell, Bob. *Favorite Greek Myths*. Dover Publications, 1996. Written specifically for middle school students.

D'Aulaire, Ingri and Edgar. *D'Aulaires' Book of Greek Myths*. Picture Yearling, 1992 (paperback); Econoclad, 1999. A beautifully illustrated collection of myths for ages 9–12.

Osbourne, Mary Pope. *Favorite Greek Myths*. Scholastic, 1991. Written at a middle school reading level, these 12 well-known Greek myths have colorful illustrations.

Russell, William F. *Classic Myths to Read Aloud*. Crown Publishers, 1992. This collection of Greek and Roman myths includes the history behind many commonly used words and phrases that originated with these myths, providing an enjoyable way to build students' cultural literacy.

Also by Christopher Paul Curtis

Bud, Not Buddy. This Newbery-award winning book tells the humorous tale of a motherless African-American boy's adventures as he searches for his unknown father during the Great Depression.

About Christopher Paul Curtis

Podell, Tim. *Good Conversations!: Christopher Paul Curtis*. Tim Podell Productions, 2000 (VHS video). A taped interview designed for children in grades 3–8 who are reading the works of Christopher Paul Curtis.

Empire State Building Web Sites

www.esbnyc.com—This is the official Internet site all about the Empire State Building. The Web site will expose students to an amazing amount of information, especially if they click on the letters FAQ (frequently asked questions).

www.nyctourist.com/empire1.htm—This Web site gives photographic views in all different directions from the Empire State Building's 86th floor outdoor observation deck. It concisely points out well-known landmarks that can be seen (e.g., Macy's and "the Flat Iron" building).

Climatic Data Web Sites

http://www.nrcc.cornell.edu/ccd.html—This is the address for Northeast Regional Climate Center, which offers comparative climatic data for cities throughout the United States.

http://www.wrh.noaa.gov/wrhq/nwspage.html—This is the address for the National Weather Service. At the site map, click on the city name, then click on Research or Climate Data.

Civil Rights Movement Web Sites

http://homeworkspot.com/high/socialstudies/civilrights.htm—Extensive collection of K–12 student reference materials.

www.educationplanet.com/search/history/United_States_History/Civil_Rights_Movement—A K–12 Web site designed to help parents, teachers, and students find quality educational resources. Has lesson plans and links to other interesting sites.

www.civilrightsmuseum.org—This is the official Web site for the National Civil Rights Museum, located in Memphis, Tennessee. There is an interesting interactive tour of the museum, but you have to go through the tour in order and it will take about 25 screens to get to the 1960s.

www.watson.org/~lisa/blackhistory—A comprehensive set of online articles detailing the entire history of the black Civil Rights movement from the Dred Scott case through 1975.

www.samford.edu/schools/artsci/history/uccp10—You may be able to read "The Ballad of Birmingham" at this Web address.

Answer Key

Page 10—Quiz Time

1. The setting of this story is Flint, Michigan, in 1963.

2. Kenny believes that his neighbors secretly call his family the Weird Watsons.

3. Byron Watson is a conceited, arrogant, mean, teenager who thinks he's too cool for the rest of his family. (any two)

4. Byron says, "Give my regards to Clark, Poindexter" whenever he's going to skip school (Clark Elementary) that day.

5. Kenny faces several problems at school. He's seen as "too smart" by many of the kids. Other kids call him Cockeye Kenny because he has a lazy eye. Larry Dunn, Byron, and Buphead bully him. Before Rufus arrives he doesn't have any real friends, either. (any two)

6. Yes, Rufus does "save" Kenny by distracting the kids from teasing Kenny. Rufus is an even easier target; or, No, the "saver" Kenny has heard about in church is a divine being, not Rufus. (Accept either answer if it is supported.)

7. Buphead is Byron's best friend and another bully.

8. Kenny and Rufus's friendship is hurt when Kenny laughs at Larry Dunn's mean remarks about the jeans that Rufus and his little brother Cody take turns wearing.

9. People who threat Kenny badly are Byron and Buphead, who throw Kenny in snowbank and spit a mouthful of water all over him; LJ, who tricks Kenny and steals a lot of his toy dinosaurs; and Larry Dunn, who takes half of the dollar that Kenny finds. (any 2)

10. You can tell Momma is a caring person because she cries when Byron is stuck to the car mirror, she packs extra sandwiches for Rufus and Cody every day for lunch, and she helps to repair Kenny's relationship with Rufus. (any 2)

11. Rufus and Cody are too poor to have a lunch, so they share Kenny's lunch every day.

12. Yes, because Bryon got Kenny's gloves back from Larry Dunn; or, no, because Bryon was abusive to Larry Dunn when he found out he'd stolen Kenny's gloves. (Accept either answer if it is supported.)

Page 13—Greek Myths

1. Zeus asked Echo to distract his wife Hera by talking to her.

2. Zeus asked Echo to do this so that Hera wouldn't notice that he was flirting with other women.

3. Hera figured out what Zeus and Echo were up to and became furious. She took away Echo's ability to speak normally, leaving her only able to repeat the last word spoken to her.

4. Echo fell in love with Narcissus because he was so handsome.

5. Narcissus rejected Echo.

6. Nemesis punished Narcissus by making him fall in love with his own reflection.

7. Echo hid in a cave and wasted away until all that remained of her was her ability to repeat the last word spoken to her.

8. Unable to move away from his beautiful reflection, Narcissus wasted away at the edge of the pool until he vanished. A yellow flower grew in the place where he had sat.

Page 15—Quiz Time

1. Joetta is Kenny's little sister.

2. Byron's "Nazi Parachutes Attack American and Get Shot Down Over the Flint River" movie goes like this: Bryon sets a toilet paper "parachute" on fire, lets it fall down into the toilet, then flushes the "Nazi" invader and salutes, saying the brave parachutist was buried at sea.

3. Joetta stops her mother from burning Bryon by blowing out every single match that Momma lights.

4. Momma is so upset about Bryon playing with matches for several reasons: she remembers her own bad experience with fire from her childhood, she doesn't want him to endanger their family by catching the house on fire, and she doesn't like that he disobeys her.

5. Kenny is surprised when he sees the popsicle-stick cross in the alley because Bryon is always bullying other children and yet feels bad enough to bury a mourning dove and make a cross for it after deliberately hitting the bird with a cookie.

6. Byron felt so bad about killing the mourning dove, he began vomiting. He hadn't meant for it to die when he hit it with a cookie. He buried the bird and made it a popsicle-stick cross as a grave marker.

7. Grandma Sands is Momma's mother, who lives in Birmingham, Alabama.

8. A butter or a conk is slang for a hairdo in which an African-American person has his or her naturally curly hair chemically straightened. Byron gets a conk to defy his parents.

9. (Allow reasonable and supported answers.)

10. (Allow reasonable and supported answers.)

11. In every one of Byron's latest fantastic adventures, he is defying adult authority.

12. Byron didn't like it; he swore when he went back in the house after he heard the news.

Answer Key *(cont.)*

Page 19—Portmanteau Words

1. squinched = squeezed + pinched
2. sniggled = snickered + giggled
3. glugging = chugging and gurgling
4. blanged = blasted + danged

Page 20—Quiz Time

1. Dad has the Ultra-Glide installed in the Brown Bomber. The Ultra-Glide is the stereo system with speakers that can play record albums in a car.
2. Dad tells Kenny the real reason that Byron is being sent to Birmingham is that he has to realize the kind of place that the world can be.
3. Momma gets ready for the trip by packing everyone's clothes in suitcases; packing a lot of food in a cooler; creating a notebook that outlines a schedule, the route, places to stop, and points of interest.
4. Mrs. Davidson gave Joetta the angel statue because she really likes Joetta and will miss her while she's in Birmingham.
5. (Allow reasonable and supported answers.)
6. (Allow reasonable and supported answers.)
7. The things that frightened Kenny and Byron at the rest stops were outhouses, snakes, and "rednecks."
8. No one wants to hold Joey's head while she's sleeping because she drools.
9. The trip would have been different because it would have taken three days. The family also would have slept one night in a motel and another night in the car.
10. Grandma Sands is nothing like Kenny expects. He expected her to be a big, rabid troll foaming at the mouth. Instead, she's a very tiny, frail, older-looking version of his own mother.
11. Momma doesn't like her mother living with a man other than her father.
12. (Allow reasonable and supported answers.)

Page 23—Figurative Language

1. metaphor	7. metaphor
2. simile	8. hyperbole
3. personification	9. hyperbole
4. hyperbole	10. simile
5. simile	11. personification
6. simile	12. metaphor

Page 24—Using a Road Atlas

2. Detroit, MI; Toledo, OH; Dayton, OH; Cincinnati, OH; Lexington, KY; Knoxville, TN; Chattanooga, TN; Gadsden, AL (any five)

3.

State	Capital
Michigan	Lansing
Ohio	Columbus
Kentucky	Frankfort
Tennessee	Nashville
Georgia*	Atlanta
Alabama	Montgomery

  *They pass through the uppermost northwest corner of Georgia for a few miles.

4. No, they did not travel through a single state capital.
5. They change from Route 75 to Route 59.
6. Birmingham, Mobile, Montgomery, Huntsville, Tuscaloosa. They are probably the largest cities in the state of Alabama.
7. From Birmingham take Route 65 north to Indianapolis, Indiana. Then get on Route 69 north and stay on it all the way to Flint, Michigan. (Allow variations if student can point them out on a map.)

Page 25—Quiz Time

1. Mr. Robert lives with Grandma Sands and is her best friend.
2. Mr. Robert impressed Kenny and Byron by telling them that he once gave mouth-to-nose resuscitation after a raccoon drowned the dog.
3. It is so hot that the Watson children only have the energy to sit around, go fishing, or go swimming.
4. Grandma Sands warns the children not to go to Collier's Landing because there's a whirlpool there that drowned a little boy.
5. (Allow reasonable and supported responses.)
6. Momma got embarrassed when her mother frankly said that things change and that Mr. Robert is now her dearest friend.
7. Kenny sees a turtle out in the deep water, and he wants to catch it for a pet.
8. Grandma Sands meant that there was a whirlpool.
9. Kenny sees the Wool Pooh as a large, gray monster with no face and big, square fingers. It grabs Kenny's legs and drags him under the surface of the water four times. No matter how hard he tries, he can't break free of its grip until Byron comes to rescue him.
10. Kenny would probably have drowned.
11. & 12. (Allow reasonable and supported responses.)

Page 28—Learning About Weather

Since climatic data is always changing and new data is being added to the Web, allow a 3°F range in the students' responses. Information inside parentheses is for your information and not to be expected in student responses.

1. The winter in Flint is typically cold (averages are all below freezing) but somewhat moderated by high humidity.

Answer Key *(cont.)*

2. The average winter temperature is 27°F (-3°C).

3. The average relative humidity in the winter is 74%.

4. The average total snowfall for the winter is 38 inches (97 cm).

5. The dangers associated with winter weather in Flint include blizzards, hypothermia, and frostbite. A blizzard is a heavy snowstorm accompanied by high winds, resulting in poor visibility. Hypothermia is such an abnormally low body temperature that it may result in death. Frostbite is frozen skin tissue (usually on extremities such as hands and feet) that often must be removed.

6. (Answers will vary.)

7. The summer in Birmingham is typically hot with high humidity. (The mean number of days with temperatures of 90°F or higher is 53 days.)

8. The average summer temperature is 78°F (26°C).

9. The average relative humidity is 72%.

10. The total amount of precipitation (rain) is about 12.5 inches (932 cm).

11. The dangers associated with summer weather in Birmingham include heat stroke, sunstroke, and dehydration. Heat stroke is a severe illness caused by exposure to extremely high temperatures. Sunstroke is heat stroke caused by being out in the sun too long. Dehydration can occur when a person sweats out more moisture than is replenished by water intake. All three conditions can be fatal. (Tornadoes typically occur in the spring; hurricanes are usually in the fall.)

12. (Answers will vary.)

Page 29—Doing Library Research

1. atlas or a map site on the Internet
2. Reader's Guide to Periodical Literature
3. microfilm (possibly microfiche) for that specific date (may only be available at metropolitan libraries)
4. atlas or map
5. almanac
6. dictionary
7. catalog of library holdings
8. Internet weather site
9. thesaurus
10. encyclopedia

Page 30—Quiz Time

1. No, Kenny doesn't tell his parents about his near drowning. (Allow reasonable and supported explanations as to why.)
2. Kenny tells Joey that she looks pretty as she leaves for Sunday school.
3. When Kenny reaches the church, he enters the building to search for Joey. He finds what he believes is her shoe.

4. Kenny flees when he sees the Wool Pooh lurking in the church's rubble.

5. Kenny doesn't want to look at Joey because he doesn't want to see her in the clutches of the Wool Pooh.

6. (Allow any reasonable responses.)

7. The World-Famous Watson Pet Hospital is located behind the couch in the Watsons' living room. The family's pets go there to hide when they are sick to see whether or not they will be cured. After Kenny returns to Flint, he hides in the World-Famous Watson Pet Hospital.

8. To lure Kenny from behind the couch, Byron tries many things. He asks Kenny to watch television with him, asks him to play ball, come out to eat, walk to Mitchell's, and come see his first facial hair. Byron even sleeps on the couch at night. (any three)

9. Kenny tells Byron that he feels ashamed because when he saw the Wool Pooh at the church he ran away rather than fight to save Joey. He feels that Byron fought the Wool Pooh to save him, yet he did not do the same for Joey.

10. Byron does not believe in the Wool Pooh, magic powers, and genies. He orders Kenny to stop talking about such things or he'll leave him to cry alone in the bathroom.

11. The Wool Pooh symbolizes fear, evil, and death to Kenny. He sees it when he is trapped in the whirlpool and also in the rubble of the bombed church.

12. (Allow reasonable and supported responses.)

Page 33—Math Word Problems

1. Byron is 3 years, 0 months, 19 days older than Kenny.
   1/16/50 to 1/16/53 = 3 years
   2/29/52 (leap day) = 1 day
   1/16/53 to 2/3/53 = 18 days

2. Kenny is 5 years, 2 months, and 27 days older than Joetta.
   2/4/53 to 2/4/58 = 5 years
   2/4/58 to 4/4/58 = 2 months
   2/29/56 (leap day) = 1 day
   4/4/58 to 4/30/58 = 26 days

3. 375 miles/29 gallons of gas = 12.93 rounded to 12.9 miles per gallon

4. Joetta slept 69% of the total trip time
   18 hours/26 hours = 0.692 x 100 = 69.2%, rounded to 69%
   Kenny slept 63% of the total trip time.
   16.5 hours/26 hours = 0.6346 x 100 = 63.46%, rounded to 63%
   Byron slept 58% of the total trip time.
   15 hours/26 hours = 0.5769 x 100 = 57.69%, rounded to 58%

© Teacher Created Materials, Inc — 47 — #3155 The Watsons Go to Birmingham—1963

Answer Key *(cont.)*

Momma slept 50% of the total trip time.

13 hours/26 hours = 0.5 x 100 = 50%

5. $81,000 loan

Insurance of $250,000 + baked goods sales of $9,000 + rummage sale of $26,000 + donations of $92,000 = $377,000 money raised

Damage – money raised = amount of loan $458,000 – $377,000 = $81,000 still needed to repair the church

Page 38

Unit Test Option I

Matching (4 points each)

1. G	3. E	5. J	7. K	9. H
2. C	4. L	6. F	8. B	10. D

True/False/Explain (4 points each)

1. False. Byron is not angry with Kenny for reading in front of his class. He tells him that the teacher ought to pay him for making him perform.

2. True

3. False. Kenny believes Rufus is his "saver." Cody is Rufus's little brother.

4. True   5. True

6. False. Byron is so upset when he kills a mourning dove that he vomits. Then he buries the dove under a handmade popsicle-stick cross.

7. False. Dad is so upset when Byron gets a conk that he shaves Byron's head.

8. True

9. False. Joey puts the angel at the bottom of her sock drawer because she doesn't like it.

10. True   11. True

12. False. Kenny can't escape from the Wool Pooh until Byron comes and helps him out of the water.

13. False. Joey wasn't hurt in the bombing; she left the church before the explosion. She had thought she saw Kenny across the street and followed him home.

14. True

15. False. Byron is the one who finally pulls Kenny out of his depression.

Page 39

Unit Test Option II

1. Kenny is using an exaggeration to say that Mr. Alums put him in "the line of fire" by having him read aloud in front of Byron's class.

2. Kenny suspected LJ wanted to steal all of his dinosaurs, but Kenny was impressed by the clever plan that LJ thought of to actually make it happen. He convinced Kenny to bury "radioactive" dinosaurs under three large rocks in his backyard. Later, LJ returned, dug up the dinosaurs and took off with them.

3. He means that Byron could be even be meaner than Larry Dunn could be. Kenny feels that Byron's treatment of Larry is worse than what Larry did (stealing Kenny's gloves and giving him a "Maytag wash" in the snow).

4. Kenny can't stand to watch Byron abuse Larry Dunn by throwing him against a metal fence, so he leaves.

5. Kenny is baffled by "Daddy Cool" (Byron). He can't understand why Byron got so upset by killing a dove when he is always callous toward other children.

6. Byron is making an analogy in which he is the "top dog." He's saying that all the little (lesser) dogs want to bite him when he's down to get back at him for all the times he's ruled over them.

7. Kenny likes the fact that his dad is talking to him man-to-man. He wants his dad to continue, and so he makes a conscious effort to not do anything childish or inappropriate.

8. Byron scares Kenny into thinking that some "rednecks" (hillbillies) want to eat African Americans for dinner. So, in Kenny's hurry to finish peeing, he gets some urine in his pants.

9. It is surprising for Kenny to see his Momma feeling like she'd been scolded (by her own mother, Grandma Sands) because Momma is Kenny's authority figure.

10. Kenny is describing how Byron is hysterical over the near drowning of his little brother. Byron was terrified that he hadn't rescued Kenny in time and couldn't stop kissing him once he found out that Kenny was alive.

11. Kenny sees the Wool Pooh in the church and thinks that he has gotten the girl to whom the shoe belonged. He suddenly realizes that the girl is dead, and he believes that it is Joey.

12. He is hiding behind the couch in the World-Famous Watson Pet Hospital, waiting to see if the magic powers there were going to cure him of his depression or just let him die. Whenever a pet died in the World-Famous Watson Pet Hospital, the parents left a crumpled-up yellow towel where the animal had been.

13. Kenny is saying that the Wool Pooh is the embodiment of death and evil, and that both of those things are frighteningly real.

14. Kenny feels certain that even though there's evil in the world, there is also goodness. He remembers feeling the presence of angels when Grandma Sands put her arms around the Watson family and was so very happy to see them.

Page 40

Unit Test Option III (20 points each)

(Answers will vary; acceptable reasonable responses.)